GINGER LOVES JOHNNY

BY
D.C. BLACKBIRD

DEDICATION

For my dad.

The kindest, most decent, most thoughtful, most wonderful man

I ever met in my life. I will never meet another man like him.

He was quite unlike anyone most people had ever met before.

He was honestly good. He was truly great.

I miss him.

STORY CONTENTS

01.   When Ginger needed Johnny.

02.   When Ginger met Johnny.

03.   When Johnny took care of Ginger.

04.   Ginger & Johnny together.

05.   When Johnny was away from Ginger.

06.   When Ginger was away from Johnny.

07.   When Johnny came home from Greece.

08.   When Johnny went to the hospital.

09.   When Johnny came home from the hospital.

10.   When Ginger came home to Johnny.

11.   When Ginger took care of Johnny.

12.   When Johnny said goodbye to Ginger.

13.   When the morning arrived.

14.   When Ginger said goodbye to Johnny.

15.   When Ginger and Johnny spoke again.

Please share this book with others. If possible, please order additional copies and give this book with anyone you know who has a good heart, who cares about other people, and especially those who care about cats & dogs and the special relationship that many humans have with their non-human companions.

It will take you roughly 25 minutes to read this entire book.

#GingerLovesJohnny

We apologize in advance for any grammatical errors. If you see any, please let us know.

Questions? email the publisher at: Cardinal@CampfireNetwork.com

GingerLovesJohnny.com

INTRODUCTION

Wow. My dad. Wow. What father on earth would not want their son to begin describing him with the word "wow"? Honestly, there is no other way. Johnny was a genuinely warm & incredibly honest man who was living in South Florida for decades, but was at heart a native New Yorker, where he was educated in areas and aspects of architecture and landscape design. He also learned to be a great chef who owned a popular restaurant in NYC. He was always interested in healthy living way before it was a fad, exercising at Jack LaLanne gyms and "working out" at home. Way before "juicing" and "protein shakes" became trendy, Johnny had his very own chain of juice bars from Palm Beach to Miami where his team sold fresh-squeezed juices and fruit smoothies from Johnny's very own recipes! Throughout his life he'd go jogging, no matter the weather, and he was never sick a day in his life!

Johnny was a man of great spiritual faith. He attended church at least once a week, and he donated his considerable cooking skills to the restaurant at the church he attended. In addition to being involved in multiple business ventures, Johnny also found time to be an inventor! In fact, he always had an assortment of creative projects going on. He did all this while maintaining wonderful, lifelong personal and professional relationships. Johnny could be trusted to always do the right thing. Truth be told, you'd be hard-pressed to find a single person anywhere in the world who has anything less than glowing words to say about Johnny. He was that special. He was as close to being an angel as anyone could expect to meet here on earth. I am so fortunate to have had a dad like Johnny. **Wow.**

1

WHEN GINGER NEEDED JOHNNY

During the autumn of 2004, Johnny received a phone call while he was home preparing one of his delicious soups, based on his own recipe. The caller asked Johnny if he wanted a dog. She was a little Maltese who had been repeatedly abandoned in a parking lot.

It was indeed a godsend that the person did not keep this newly-found dog and offered her to Johnny, who eagerly accepted.

Johnny called to tell me the good news. I was excited for my dad. In fact, since I had friends in the area where the dog was found, I arranged to go down there and transport the little innocent angel to my dad.

My dad loved dogs, but he hadn't had one in a long while. My dad had a lot of time and love and energy to share. This was going to be the beginning of a great new chapter in my dad's wonderful life.

2

When
Ginger
Met
Johnny

The little Maltese dog needed a home, but more than that, she needed a loving home. She needed a bath. She needed her teeth to be cleaned. She needed to be brought to a vet. She needed to be put on a proper diet. She needed kindness and affection. She needed love. This little angel needed Johnny, and he did not let her down.

Yes! This tiny, young dog was so happy to finally have the type of home that she deserved and dreamed of. She took an instant liking to Johnny, as if they were destined to meet and fall in love with one another.

There was a kind of magic between them that radiated in the air when they were together. This was not just a man with his dog, or a dog with her human, this was something that mere words simply can not describe. You'd have to see it to believe it. I am sure you know what I am talking about. It was love at first sight.

He named her **Ginger.**

3

WHEN JOHNNY TOOK CARE OF GINGER

Johnny got Ginger a nice comfy bed. Johnny got Ginger some wonderful toys. Johnny took Ginger for long and leisurely walks through his – their – neighborhood. Together they went out each morning, as the sun rose over South Florida. Together they went out each night, as the moon hovered in the dark skies above.

Johnny trained Ginger. She could lay down. She could sit up. She could roll over. She could break dance! She could even talk. In fact, they even had a game they played. Johnny would say ...

"Johnny loves Ginger."

"Johnny loves Ginger."

"Johnny loves Ginger."

While he spoke Ginger would look up at him and would wag her tail and her eyes would sparkle.

Then Johnny would say, "Who does Ginger love?" In reply, Ginger would bark 5 times.

BARK BARK. BARK. BARK BARK.

She was clearly saying ...

"Ginger loves Johnny!"

4

GINGER &
JOHNNY
TOGETHER

Ginger and Johnny spent all their time together.

In the daytime, Ginger would stay near Johnny while he worked in his home office.

In the evenings, Ginger would sit on the sofa with Johnny while he read, studied, designed gardens, invented, and warched TV.

The only time that Ginger sat far away was when Johnny was exercising. After all, she would not want a dumbbell to fall on her pretty little head.

At night, Ginger would sleep on the bed with Johnny.

Ginger liked it when it was cool outside. Johnny would often tell Ginger about snow, and promised he would take her up north someday so she could feel snowflakes on her pure white fur.

In addition to spending all their days and nights together at home, Johnny also took Ginger with him when he went to visit me and my family.

Ginger did not like other dogs (well, maybe a couple), but she did like our cats. After all, they were her cousins!

5

POSTCARD

Welcome to GREECE

Athens GREECE

WHEN JOHNNY WAS AWAY FROM GINGER

During August, 2017 Johnny made plans to leave the USA for the first time. One of his friends offered him an all-expense paid trip to Greece. Who could turn that down?

Johnny told me that he had some hesitation about leaving Ginger with his ex-neighbor for so long because he was elderly and had some health issues. Even though I lived relatively far away, I offered to take care of Ginger.

Just at this time, Johnny's best friend of 60+ years became ill, so Johnny was hesitant to leave the country so he could care for his friend. Soon Johnny was assured by others - myself included - that his friend would be looked after, and that we would be available to help if something were to happen to his friend, or if anything happened to the elderly ex-neighbor who would be caring for Ginger.

Hesitantly, Johnny left Ginger for the first time.

Unfortunately, just a day after arriving in Greece, Johnny's best friend passed away. His name was Alex. He was like an Uncle to me.

My dad called me from Greece to let me know. He said he was exhausted from the flight, and was upset about his best friend. I told him to come home, and he considered doing so, while also being told by others that there was nothing he could do about his best friend, and that he should get some rest and try to clear his mind and enjoy himself, as his best friend would have wanted him to. But my dad was not that kind of person. He couldn't just forget about the loss of his best friend and suddenly start having fun. Despite the endless interesting and historic attractions that could be seen everywhere, my dad spent the rest of his time in Greece being terribly unhappy.

My dad told me he used to walk along the beach and look up at the sky. He would say ...

"Johnny loves Ginger."

And he told me he would imagine hearing Ginger barking in reply.

"Ginger loves Johnny."

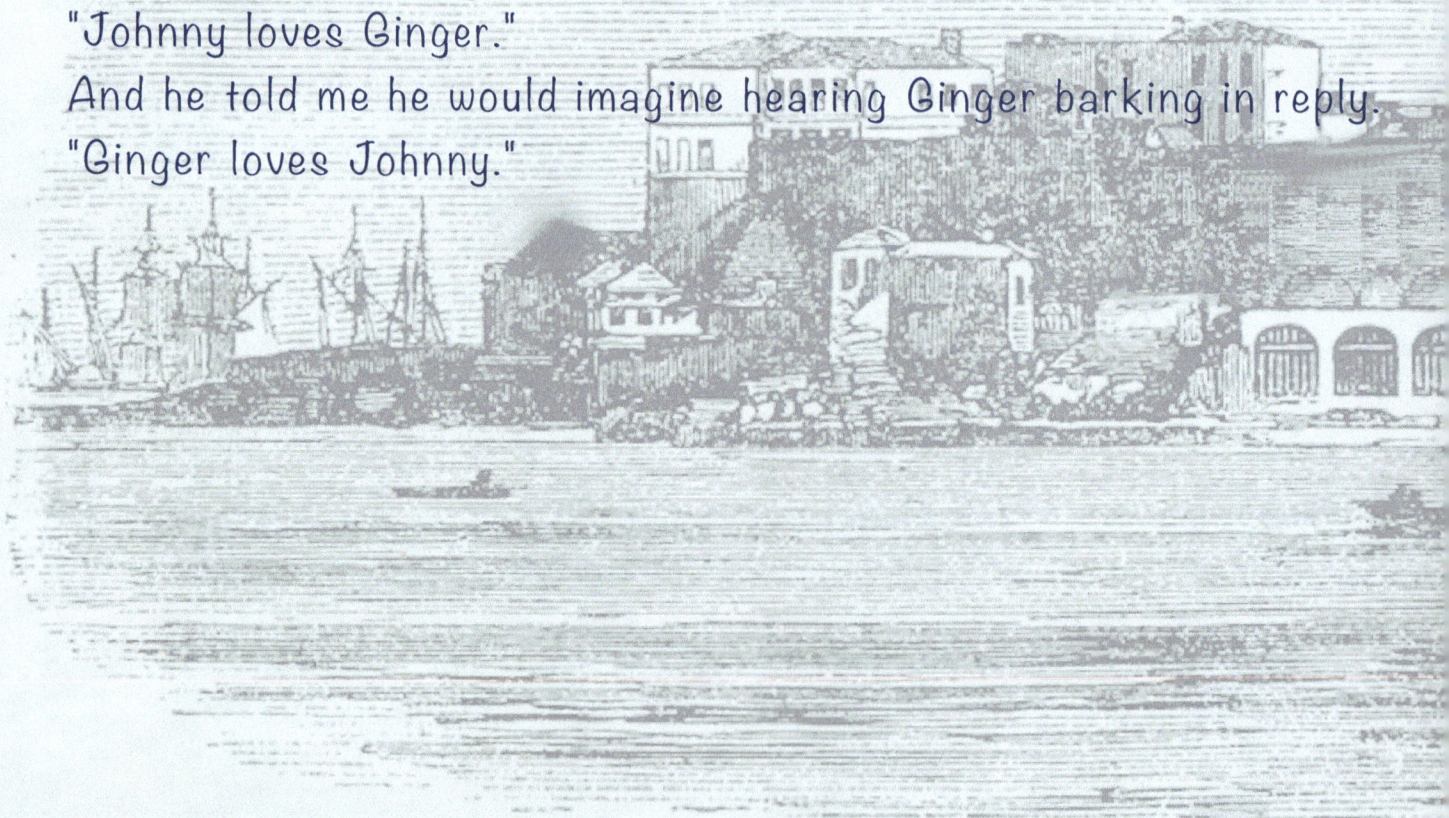

6

WHEN GINGER WAS AWAY FROM JOHNNY

Sadly, Ginger was unhappy, too. Sure, she was in a safe environment, but she was denied the love and affection of her beloved human daddy who had taken care of her for so long. She missed the smell of her own home, and her own toys, and her own things. She missed Johnny.

I was told that there were times when she would look up at the sky, and Ginger would bark 5 times.

BARK BARK. BARK. BARK BARK.

She was clearly saying ...

"Ginger loves Johnny."

Perhaps she heard Johnny talking to her from across the ocean when he was in Greece.

Yes. I bet she did.

7

WHEN JOHNNY CAME HOME FROM GREECE

At the end of August, 2017, after three weeks abroad, Johnny returned to the USA, and to his home, and to Ginger. They were both so happy to be back together. I was happy he was home, too.

Unfortunately, Johnny was not the same. He was terribly stressed out from the trip. He was depressed over losing his best friend. He was also upset that other people were supposedly trying to claim his best friend's possessions. He was also exhausted from the long flight home.

He was concerned that his business had been neglected for so long, and he tried to catch up to where he left off.

Days went by and Johnny was not feeling any better. Because Johnny had never been sick before in his entire life he did not know what was normal - or not normal. He was told he was probably just tired and dehydrated and he should just get plenty of rest and drink a lot of water. So he did that.

I finally convinced my dad to get a friend to take him to the hospital to figure out what was wrong. I was thinking perhaps he had a parasite from food or drinking the water overseas. After all, Johnny wouldn't be the first to get sick after such an exraordinary trip. He was reluctant to go to the doctor, however. He never really had to depend upon a doctor for medical advice before. He was also reluctant after hearing so many horror stories of doctors being wrong about so much so many times.

Despite all this, Johnny went to a hospital where, after a brief evaluation, he was told he was fine. My dad called me when he was on his way home. He sounded great. I was relieved until he told me that they didn't check him for a parasite or Hepatitis, or much else. I told him to go to another hospital, but he said he just wanted to go back home and get some rest and spend time with Ginger. He felt bad that he had not been able to spend much time with her.

So Johnny went home after being told he would be fine, but he was not fine. He was clearly sick and he was not getting better. He had bizarre symptoms. For example, Johnny smelled something horrible, that only he could smell. He said it smelled like the apartment of his best friend who had died in August. I wondered if that was perhaps Psychosomatic as a result of depression from losing his best friend.

I told him to go see another doctor, or two or three! He made some appointments. One was going to be a week away, another was going to be two weeks away. I told him that was not good enough, and he needed some serious tests done immediately, but he felt that he was likely suffering from exhaustion and stress, and he wanted to spend more time at home, and with Ginger. He said she made him feel better. I certainly knew that was true.

After his doctor appointments came and went I asked him what he was told, and he said he could not remember. I asked him how that was possible. Didn't he take notes? Wasn't a friend with him? He said the doctors said things he did not understand, that they were reading off test results, and it was not possible to remember all that stuff, but basically they said they didn't know what was wrong, and that they needed him to go for even more tests.

I told him I was going to come see him immediately, but he told me to wait until the next tests were done, and that he was doing okay, and was feeling a little bit better because many of his symptoms seemed to be going away.

But I was tired of being in the dark, and not knowing what was going on, so - without telling my dad - I booked a flight to fly down to Florida to see him at his next doctor's appointment. I arrived at Ft. Lauderdale International Airport, rented a car, and drove straight to the hospital.

When I arrived it took me awhile to figure out how to navigate through that massive place, but I finally found my dad. He looked weak, thin & tired, but not nearly as bad as I was led to believe. He was still walking, and seemed strong. He was very surprised and happy when he saw me. The look on his face was priceless. I am so glad I did it. I can see the look on his face right now. Classic! I told my dad that I was there to find out what was going on. I asked him to give the doctor permission to talk to me - alone. He did so, and the nurse led me into another room to wait for the doctor, while my dad sat in the waiting room with his friend.

When the doctor entered the room I explained that I was very frustrated, and that I wanted to know what was going on with my dad. The doctor said he was not sure, so they were going to run some more tests. At that point I asked the doctor point blank if Johnny's condition was terminal.

"Does my dad have Cancer?"

The doctor looked at me as if I was the dumbest guy on earth. He said, "No. Your father doesn't have Cancer. If he did his white blood cells would be elevated, and he would have many other symptoms that he does not have. So don't worry about that."

Relieved, I went out to see my dad. His friend seemed glad that I was there, and he said he wanted to go home, and since I was there he could now do that. I don't even remember if he said goodbye or not. He just quickly turned and left us. It was a good thing I had a rental car. My dad asked me how long I was staying and I replied, "I bought a one way ticket. I'll stay here as long as you need me."

He said, "You are in the middle of a lot of work. Go do that. I'll be fine."

I said, "Nothing is more important than you, dad. Taking care of you is my job now. Everything else can wait."

Johnny smiled. Even though we had not seen each other much over the last couple of years, we spoke on the phone almost daily, oftentimes several times in a day. After all, we had the same interests and we liked to talk to each other. We had the same sense of humor. We liked the same movies. We liked the same music. We thought alike. We spoke alike. We were friends. My dad was my friend. I was his friend.

So after a few brief stops (my father actually leased a car that day!) and then going food shooping, I took my dad back home. He went to sleep almost immediately. In the days that followed, all the symptoms he had seemed to be dissipating. Johnny was feeling much better. Ginger being there certainly helped. She followed him around wherever he went. The three of us spent all of our time together.

But he was still tired, and I insisted that he continue going to the doctors to find out what was going on. He agreed.

Since I flew down so abruptly, and only had the clothes I was wearing and a few things in a backpack, it was agreed that I would go back home, and then return as soon as Johnny got some test results a couple of days later. With friends and neighbors there, what could possibly go wrong in a few days?

While I was gone one of his neighbors called me. My dad's legs had swollen up and he was brought to the hospital. The doctors said he had developed jaundice, and they put a stent in his liver in order to alleviate it.

I called my dad at the hospital and told him I was coming back down. He told me to hold off because they were going to do a biopsy on a benign mass that had years ago been found near his liver. He also told me that they were going to perform a colonoscopy. All of this seemed like good news in the sense that my dad was finally getting proper, 24/7 treatment for his ailments. The general consensus was that he was suffering from exhaustion, and that he had jaundice, and that he was now healing. My dad was going to be okay!

Johnny soon returned home, and so did Ginger.

Once again, I flew down to see him, and help him in any way I could. He looked better, but was still very tired. Even still, we went shopping, we went out for healthy meals, we got fresh, cold-pressed juices, we walked around the mall together, and Johnny, Ginger and I spent a lot of time in the lovely Asian-style garden my dad designed and created in his backyard. Johnny and Ginger loved it there.

Johnny would talk to Ginger, have her sit, stand, beg, roll over, and break dance. And then Johnny would say ...

"Johnny loves Ginger."

"Johnny loves Ginger."

"Johnny loves Ginger."

While he spoke Ginger would look up at him and would wag her tail and her eyes would sparkle. Then Johnny would say, "Who does Ginger love?" And Ginger would bark 5 times.

BARK BARK. BARK. BARK BARK.

She was clearly saying ...

"Ginger loves Johnny."

Since my dad was stable (and even beginning to exercise and lift weights again!) he assured me that it was okay for me to zoom up to Manhattan for a quick business meeting. I told him it could wait, but he told me he wanted me to go. He was excited about the project I was working on, and he wanted me to complete it.

He said, "You're a good son. I'm very proud of you. I'm going to be okay now. Go ahead. Tell me all about it when you come back."

Reluctantly, I left my dad. But at the time, he seemed okay. Or at least that's what I thought. What did I know? I have never been around anyone that sick before. I had no idea what was normal or not normal. Unless one deals with sick people all the time, then who does?

8

When Johnny Went to the Hospital

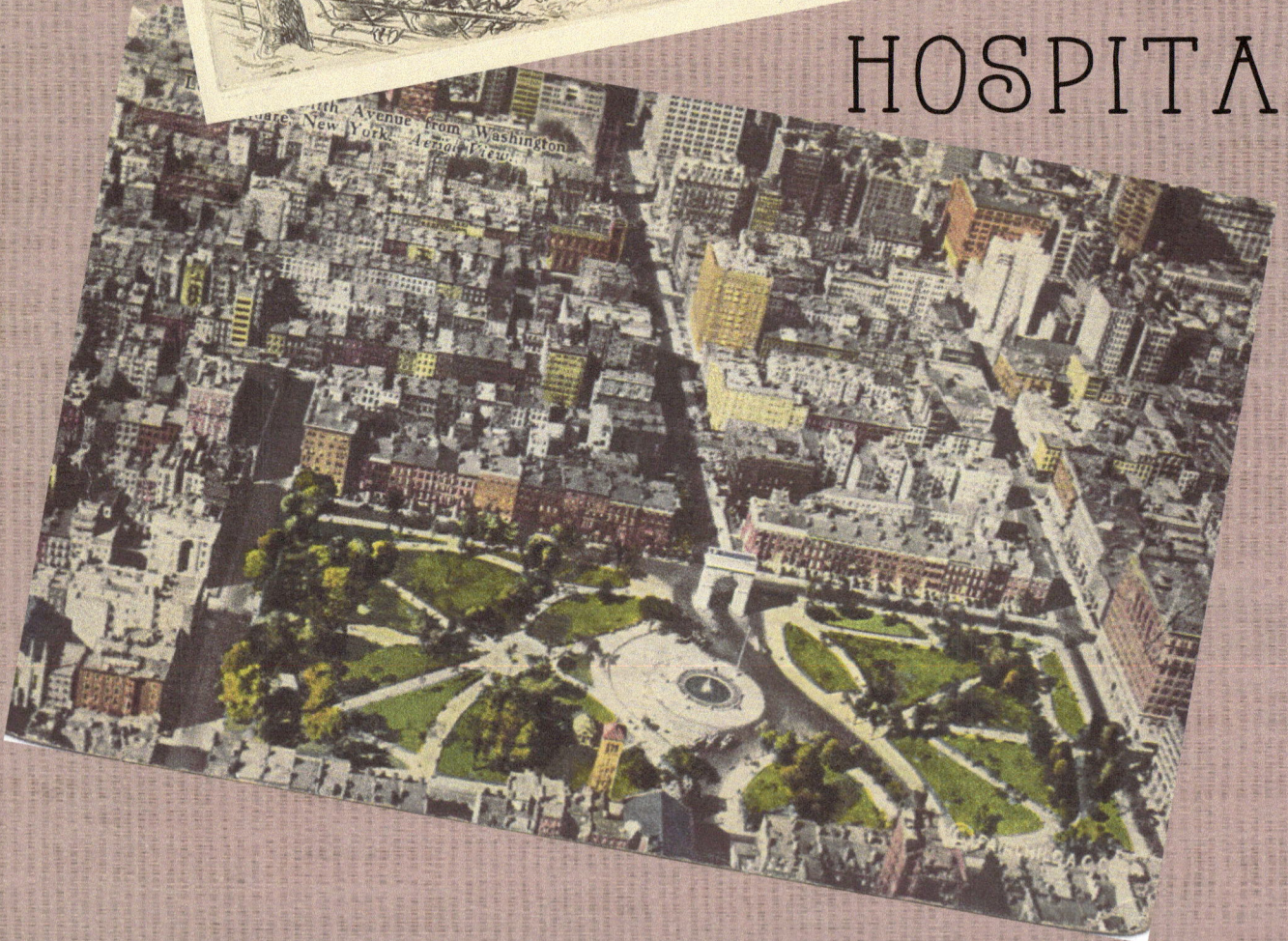

On November 1st, 2017, I was in Washington Square Park in Manhattan. I had been calling my dad all day but he was not answering. I assumed he was sleeping so I did not worry too much, but by that evening I was worried so I started calling his neighbors. I reached one of them and I asked if she could please go and check on my dad. She refused to go over there by herself because she said she "didn't want to be the one to find him," so she wanted someone to go with her. I told her I was going to call 911 and I asked if she could kindly go there and at least open the door for EMS, since she had a key. I hung up and called 911.

One of his neighbors called to tell me that when EMS arrived, Johnny was unconscious. I told him to tell my dad not to worry, and that I was on my way. I remained as calm as I could, but was a bit frantic. There was a lot to do.

I immediately made plans to head out to JFK and to fly down to Ft Lauderdale. So much of what followed is a montage in my mind. I remember running from Madison Square Garden to Port Authority to catch a bus. I remember the bus being stuck in horrible traffic and I did not think I would make it to the airport on time. I remember the bus stopping at the terminal and running as fast as I could to the entry gates, and then walking as briskly as I could through the terminal. I remember making it to the gates practically out-of-breath. I remember staring into space while on the plane and seeing one of the flight attendants looking at me, and it was then that I realized I had tears on my face.

I don't remember landing in Ft. Lauderdale. I don't remember calling an Uber driver, or the ride to the hospital, but I do remember shutting the door to the car, and running into the emergency room, and being told where my dad was, and running through the empty corridors, and hitting the elevator button, and then stepping out and walking as quickly as I could down the long, cold, sterile hall until I found my dad's room.

I remember walking in and seeing my dad, who had always been so strong, healthy, vibrant, and happy, now completely motionless, under the covers, in the bed, with IVs in his arms, and surrounded by metal boxes filled with monitoring equipment. He looked like he was ... sleeping. Yes, he was sleeping. Thankfully, he was just sleeping.

It was around midnight, I think. Maybe it was earlier in the night. Maybe it was 1 o'clock in the morning. I had no idea then, and I have no idea now. I didn't care. I put down my carry-on bag. I pulled up a chair. I approached my dad and held his hand. Warm. Good. He seemed to have a nice warm glow. He looked like he would be all right now. He was safe, and in a place where he could get the help he clearly needed.

I said. "It's okay, dad. I'm here. Everything is going to be **33**
fine. Don't worry about a thing. We are going to get through this
together."

No response. He was clearly exhausted.

I kissed him on the cheek.

His mouth moved a little bit. He knew I was there.

I whispered, "Can you look at me, dad?"

He opened his eyes and looked at me.

I said, "You're going to be okay. I promise. Don't worry."

He nodded his head gently.

I added, "You agree with that, right?"

He nodded again.

Without missing a beat I said, "Dad, I want you to look me in the
eyes and say, 'I'm going to be okay.'"

His lips moved. His mouth opened slightly, and though his voice
was dry, and his words cracked a bit, and he spoke barely above a
whisper, he looked me in the eyes and said, "I'm going to be okay."

I said, "That's right. You will be. I'm here. I'm not leaving here,
dad. You are going to be okay, dad. I promise. Don't worry about
a thing. You'll be fine."

Johnny nodded in agreement and then fell back to sleep.

A nurse walked in and asked if I was going to stay. When I told
her I would, she said she would bring me a pillow and a blanket. I

sat on the chair next to the bed and looked at my dad. He was exhausted. I was exhausted, too. I fell asleep sitting up in the chair.

At least 2 or 3 times during the night my dad and I were repeatedly startled when the BEEP BEEP BEEP alarms continually went off to alert the nurses that the DRIPS were out and needed to be replaced. How anyone can get any rest at a hospital is beyond comprehension. At one point a couple of nurse's assistants came in and woke my dad up because they had to change the sheets at whatever hour in the early morning it was.

I was glad that I was there when the sun rose so I could open the shades and let light into the room.

I was glad I was there so my dad could see a friendly face when he awoke.

I was glad that I was there to feed my dad who was too weak to eat on his own.

I was glad I was there to speak with the nurses and doctors who periodically came by during their rounds.

I was glad I stayed with my father constantly.

My dad was also glad I was there. He needed me. In fact, with the exception of showering, I stayed in the hospital room with my dad all day and slept in that chair every single day and night ... and day and night ... and day and night ... and day and night ... and day and night ... and day and night ... and day and night ... and day and night ... and day and night for the first half of November.

We spoke a lot. We laughed a bit. I could always make my dad laugh. Most of all, I kept him positive. I filled Johnny's marvelous mind with a million magnificent memories. I spoke of things we did together while I was growing up. I talked about places we went, and I reminded him of funny stories & events. We also talked a lot about Ginger. One day, while he was getting tests done, I went to his house and got some photos of Ginger to put around him. That made him smile. Sometimes when he was falling asleep I would hear him say, "Johnny loves Ginger ..."

Even though he was weak, and could barely get words out, it was important enough for him to say that, so he made the effort. It made him feel better. It put happy thoughts in his head. That is why a moment later, with his his eyes still closed, he would ask, "Who does Ginger love?"

I would then watch his face as he seemed to be listening for her bark, and he seemed to hear her, because he would smile as he would drift back asleep into his delightful dreams where Johnny and Ginger could spend enchanting time together, walking and running through grassy fields where the sun shined down all around them.

9

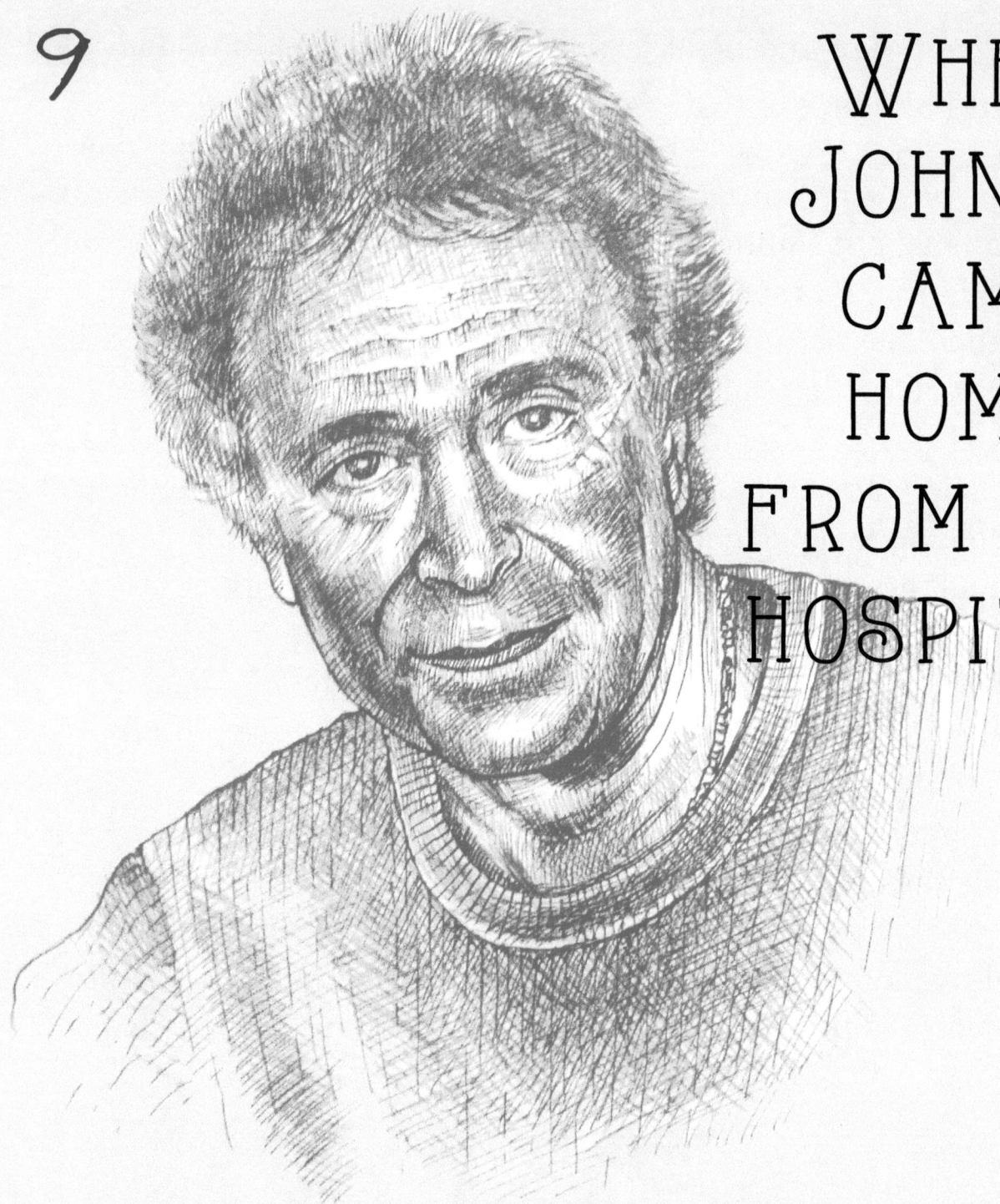

WHEN
JOHNNY
CAME
HOME
FROM THE
HOSPITAL

After we spent what seemed like an endless stream of monotonous days and nights in the hospital, the leading Hematologist came in to meet Johnny. He sat down and said, "I haven't been wrong much in my career, but I've been wrong twice lately, and both times were about you. When you first arrived in the emergency room we assumed you had three hours to live. Your Calcium levels were incompatable with life. But then you lived past that. We then assumed you'd live for a few days. There was no way someone in your condition could possibly survive. But then you lived past that." He then paused for a moment while he looked over my dad, and then confidently said, "And you've been healing. Medically, it doesn't make any sense." Another pause. He then said, "Someone is looking out for you, Johnny. At this point, I would normally tell someone in your condition that you don't have much longer. Maybe 6 weeks at the most. The problem is you were diagnosed with a benign mass in your liver many years ago, and it has grown. It has been pushing against your bile ducts. You have some toxicity that has built up. It's been causing problems. We can't do a biopsy because we are afraid that if you start bleeding we won't be able to stop it. But there may be ways to take care of this. But you need to be strong, and you are not strong right now. So I want you to go home and get stronger. I want you to eat and to put on some weight. I want you to walk into my office in two weeks, around Thanksgiving, and let's talk about how to get that mass out of you."

During this entire time I was holding my dad's hand. I was periodically looking at my dad while he was taking this all in. He did not break down. He was not upset. He was not afraid. He just looked straight ahead, nodded his head, and stayed strong. My dad was that way. He was a man of great and sincere faith. In my dad's silence during all those days I have no doubt that he was praying for strength and assistance. He believed that his prayers would be answered, but he did not leave his healing solely in the hands of another. He was ready to do his part as well. He was ready for a challenge. He knew he could do this. Most of all, he knew I was there to help him.

After the doctor left, we made plans to get my dad home.

Johnny wanted to eat in his own home.

Johnny wanted to sleep in his own home.

Johnny was eager to get on his own phone and make some calls.

Johnny wanted to see Ginger again.

So, after a short stopover at a local care center while equipment was delivered and set up in the living room, Johnny returned home.

Finally. Now we could concentrate on getting Johnny better.

10

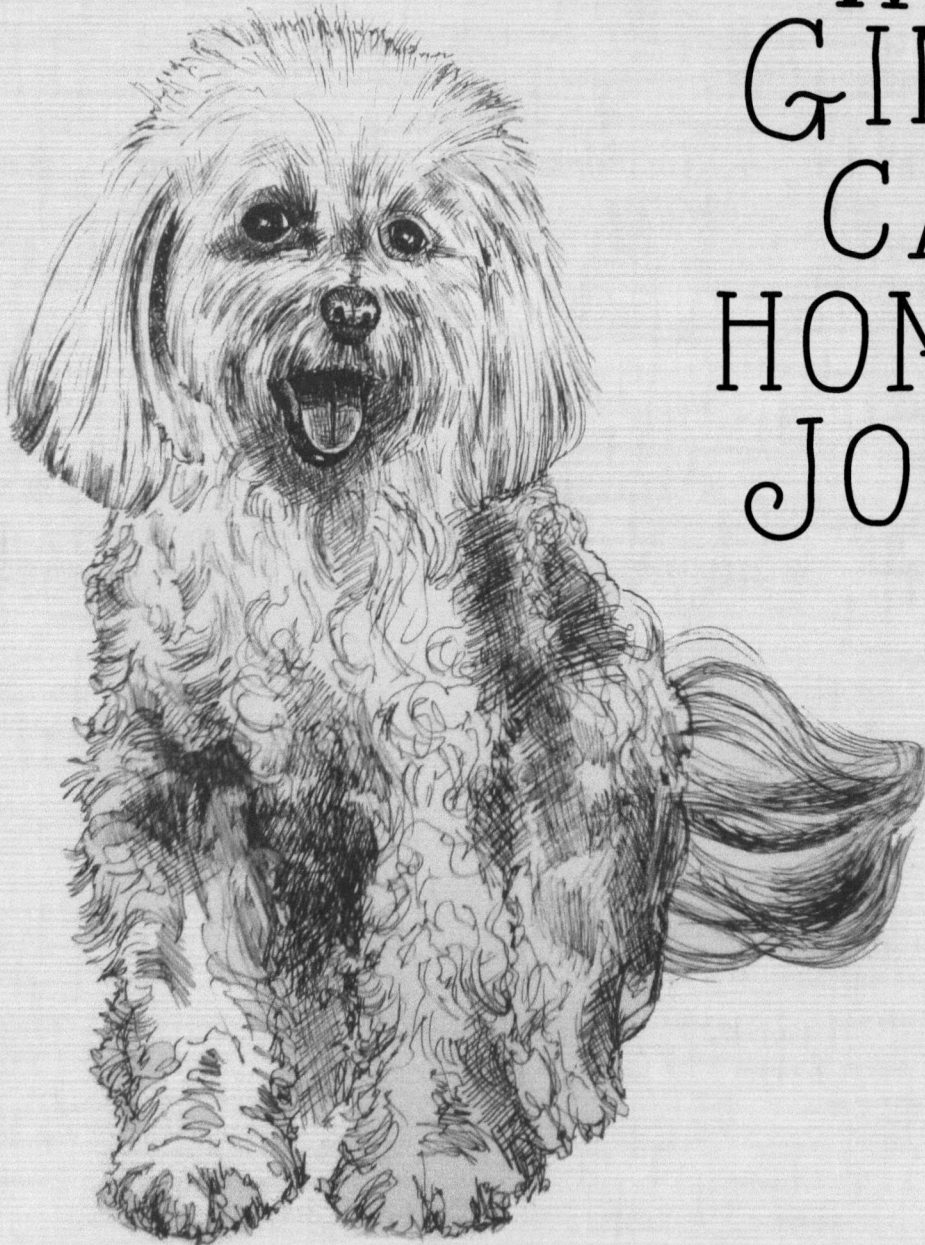

When Ginger Came Home to Johnny

Once at Johnny's home, my dad asked me to call his ex-neighbor and have him bring Ginger back home immediately. Johnny needed to get better and he needed those who loved him to be there for him.

Interestingly, Johnny wanted to get back to work in his home office. I told him he needed to stay in bed and get better. We got him an iPad for him so he could check his emails, and we also got some other items in order to make it easier for him to conduct some business from bed. He asked me to help him with his business while he was recovering and I promised I would do that, too. After all, I have helped him with many of his businesses countless times, and I knew them well. Throughout his entire life, my dad always liked to stay busy. It had a great business mind and a lot of creativity!

It took a few phone calls, but Johnny's ex-neighbor finally agreed to bring Ginger back home. The ex-neighbor walked into the house and went straight over to Johnny.

While he did so I went into the kitchen to prepare lunch for my dad. A moment later I heard the front door shut. I looked over at my dad who was all alone. Johnny was deep asleep, after having engaged in physical therapy hours earlier. I looked around and did not see Ginger. I ran to the front door and saw the ex-neighbor walking away with Ginger. I went after him and said, "Where are you going?"

Ex-neighbor: "Johnny said I could keep Ginger if anything happened to him."

Me: "What? Nothing happened to him. He's just sleeping."

Ex-neighbor: "He's not going to survive. He's dying, and he said I can keep Ginger."

Me: "First of all, my dad is NOT dying. Second, my dad tells everyone they can have Ginger. If you know my dad, then you know he jokes around like that. Heck, he even offered to give me away a few times. He loves her and everyone knows it."

Ex-neighbor: "He said I can have her if anything happened to him!"

Me: "Nothing happened to him. He's sleeping. And besides that, she is the family dog. She's not a painting. Now give me Ginger."

The ex-neighbor then turned and started to walk away.

Me: "Stop where you are. Are you out of your mind? Give me Ginger or I swear I'm going to call the police. Ginger belongs to my dad. She belongs in her own home."

The ex-neighbor kept walking, so I called the police. I followed him to his car, which he suspiciously parked down the street. I told the dispatcher the make and model of the car, it's color, and license plate number. The ex-neighbor stopped where he was. He did not know what to do. The dispatcher told me to not approach

him and to go back to my dad's house and meet the police there.
I did just that. A few police officers arrived within minutes. I met the police officers at Johnny's house and brought them inside. I showed them that my dad was in bed and sick and I showed them the shelf of photos of Ginger along the wall.

One of the officers looked at me and said, "I understand. Don't worry. I'll bring your dad's dog back."

I stayed with my dad for the next twenty minutes while the police tried to work everything out. Interestingly, Johnny's ex-wife happened to be there at the time. She went with the police to make sure that the neighbor did not leave with Ginger. She told the police that Ginger belonged to my dad and he did not give Ginger away.

Because I did not want to upset him, I did not wake my dad to tell him what was going on. At this point he had been sleeping a lot. Unfortunately, he was barely eating and drinking. I did not lose hope, though. He had a doctor's appointment in less than 10 days and I was determined he would walk in through the doctor's door and amaze everyone! We were so confident, he even asked me to get him some new clothes because he had lost so much weight. I agreed. The nurses also told me it was a good idea that my dad wear nice, clean clothes in order to make him feel better about himself - especially since friends of his were often visiting. I told him that he just needed to get some rest, and eat, and get walking again. We would do all of that. We were sure of it. But for now, my dad just looked beautiful laying there. He was so calm. So serene. So hopeful.

Awhile later the front door of Johnny's house opened. All three of the police officers walked in. One kind officer was carrying Ginger.

They all approached Johnny's bed and Ginger was handed to me. My heart felt like it skipped a beat and then melted. Ginger sniffed the air around her. She was so happy to be home. I put her down on the bed and she jumped on my dad's chest, immediately waking him up.

Like a miracle, Johnny's eyes opened wider than I'd seen them in a very long time.

Johnny smiled a big, bright, beautiful smile, and in a clear, wonderful, lyrical voice he said, "Hey, little girl!"

Wow.

It was the most amazing sight anyone could ever see. It was beautiful! It was amazing!

If you asked me for every single dime I have in the bank, and every dime I will ever earn in my life, and to give you everything I own, and to give up twenty years off my own life, in order to put that look on my father's face I would have given it to you in one second! There isn't anything I wouldn't have given you. There was no price too high to pay for what we witnessed.

But it didn't cost me anything. It didn't have to. Ginger was able to give Johnny that priceless look for free.

Wow.

It was a miracle.

I turned to the officers and said, "I know you guys deal with a lot. I know you deal with horrible and miserable people and situations all the time. I just want to thank you for this. You did something wonderful. Thank you so much. Thank you."

The police officers smiled and nodded to me and my dad and then left the house.

I turned back to my dad. He was as happy as anyone could ever be.

His voice sounded as clear as it ever had before. Loud. Crisp. Perfect! He said, "Johnny loves Ginger!"

Ginger barked.

"Ginger loves Johnny!"

If there was anything in the world that was every 100% true, it was certainly obvious to anyone and everyone that Johnny Loved Ginger and Ginger Loved Johnny.

Wow.

11 WHEN GINGER TOOK CARE OF JOHNNY

The amount of energy it must have taken for my dad to open his eyes, and to smile so wide, and to talk to Ginger as if he did not have a care in the world must have taken super human energy. In fact, it exhausted Johnny to a tremendous extent because he could barely keep his eyes open. Ginger stayed on Johnny's chest and just stared at him. It was clear how much these two loved each other.

When Johnny fell back asleep Ginger walked her little paws off of Johnny's chest and spread herself along side his left arm.

For the next few days she did not want to eat or go for a walk. Ginger wanted to take care of Johnny as Johnny had taken care of Ginger for so many years. My dad was so delighted to wake up and see and feel Ginger there. Just think - my dad's ex-neighbor tried to deprive my dad & Ginger of these priceless moments! I reassured my dad not to worry about Ginger. At that point, I was already taking care of her, and I promised him I would continue to do so. It was a lot of work, but it was fine with me. It was my honor.

I continued to spend my days and nights in the chair next to my dad's bed. Like me, Ginger refused to leave him. But unlike me, Ginger was able to sleep. I wanted - and needed - to be awake in case my dad needed me. So I often went days without sleep.

With love coming from Ginger on his left, and love coming from me on his right, my dad had a treasure that few men on earth will ever experience. We were a team. There was no way we could lose.

Dad.

Can you hear me, Dad?

Don't worry, dad.

Ginger and I are here.

Dad.

Dad?

You're going to be okay, dad.

12

WHEN
JOHNNY
SAID
GOODBYE
TO
GINGER

As the seemingly-endless days and silentious nights went by, my dad got quieter and more fatigued. I had no family helping me, but I did have nurses coming and going to do things I could not do.

I spoke to doctors and friends about options. The hospitals would not take him because there wasn't anything they could do except keep him on machinery. Even though there were progressive treatment centers, I found out they either did not take insurance, or they would not take Johnny because he was never diagnosed with cancer. Also, Johnny did not want to leave his home. I offered to take him anywhere in the world, but he would not go. He wanted to stay home and recover.

Every once and awhile Johnny motioned me close to him and he whispered the words that a father says to a son. No one will ever know what he said except him and I, but I will tell you that I often replied, "It's going to be all right, dad. Don't worry. You're going to be fine. I'm here. Ginger is here. We love you. We are here for you. You are going to be okay."

He would always nod his head in agreement. But on November 21, 2017 he used as much strength as he could muster to move his fingers along Ginger's head. He turned and looked at her and she looked back. She seemed to understand what he was thinking. He smiled and nodded to her. He whispered low, but she heard him.

13

WHEN
THE
MORNING
ARRIVED

In the early hours of the next day, while darkness was consumed by light, Johnny's heartbeat was getting weaker and weaker.

Ginger slid her little head under Johnny's hand. His fingers moved slightly, feeling her warm, fluffy fur.

I looked at my dad's face. Though he was 75 years old and never had any cosmetic procedure whatsoever, he did not have a single wrinkle on his face. It was smooth as silk and my dad seemed to glow. He looked absolutely radiant and beautiful. He seemed to be younger than me. He could have been my younger brother. He could have been my son. He had a sort of ethereal and celestial luminance that is reserved only for heavenly angels.

With the gallant strength of a valiant hero, Johnny then looked up at me and whispered. I looked into his eyes, and with all the strength left in him he said, "I'm going to be fine."

I nodded my head and maintained my composure.

My dad had a look of total serenity on his face. Whatever it was that he was praying for this entire time, he clearly believed that his prayers were answered. He had everything he ever wanted.

Even then I would not give up hope, so I am not sure what I meant when I said, "I know, dad. You're going to be fine."

But since he was a man of such great faith, I think I now realize what he truly meant. He was going to be fine. He believed it.

14

WHEN GINGER
SAID GOODBYE
TO JOHNNY

I looked down at Ginger. She would not move from my dad's arm. She kept her head under his hand and looked somber.

I put my hand on top of my dad's hand as the warmth left it, and then I put my hand on Ginger, and then I put my hand on my dad's shoulder.

The nurse checked his heartbeat. She then left us in order to make her calls.

It was then that I realized that music was playing. It had been playing for days. I stayed where I was as some of my dad's favorite songs filled the house, which was, at the same time, quieter than it had ever been. Without my dad's voice, it was silent as the heavens.

5 minutes. 30 minutes. 60 minutes. 2 hours.

I was sitting on the floor the entire time with my hand on my dad's shoulder. Every once and awhile I felt tears roll down and then off my face. It kept hitting me in waves.

I did not want to leave him. I maintained my vigil because that is what a man does. That is what a son does. That is what any good child does. That's the deal. Too many parents around the world have been all alone at the very end of their lives. I did not want my dad to be alone. But yet, I was all alone. I had no one there to talk to, and I had no one there to help, but that was okay. I was there for my dad, and that's all that mattered.

But my dad was gone.

Don't worry

I'm going to all right

I love you

Johnny Loves Ginger

Don't worry

I'm going to all right

The
doorbell
rang . . .

I ignored the bell for a long while, but the nurse opened the door and I could hear strangers enter my dad's home. They were there to take him away from Ginger and I. We both knew that as soon as we left we would never see him ever again. That would be it.

After a long while of watching a million images of my dad and I flashing through my mind I stood up. I couldn't feel my legs. My entire body felt frozen. It was as if ice water was pumping through me instead of blood. I couldn't feel my own heartbeat.

Rays of morning light wandered their way through the shades and landed gently upon my dad's serene and noble face.

I leaned over and hugged my dad tight. "I'm so sorry I wasn't able to save you, dad. I really tried." Some of my tears fell upon his face. "You had a great life. You are so loved. You're the best."

I kissed my dad's cold cheek three times. **COLD.** I told myself it was winter. I was just a kid kissing my dad after we were playing in the snow, and that thought shuttled me back in time, to such a moment when that was true. So many years ago.

Out of a force of habit, I heard myself saying. "It's going to be okay, dad. Don't worry about a thing. You're going to be fine."

I then gently moved my dad's hand and lifted Ginger up, and carried her out the back door with me.

We didn't look back.

I'll take care of Ginger, dad.

Don't worry.

Can you hear me, Dad?

We miss you.

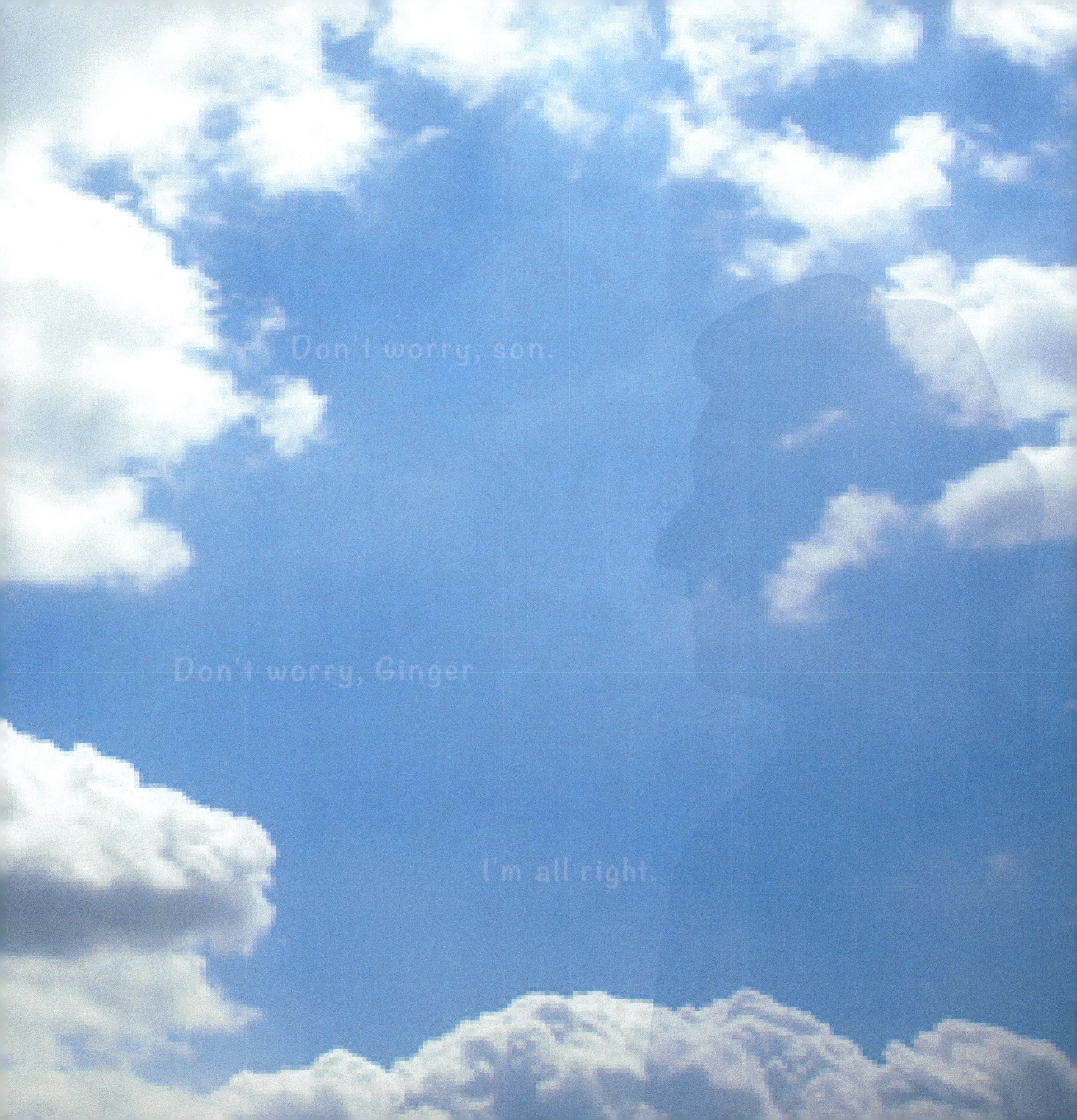

Don't worry, son.

Don't worry, Ginger

I'm all right.

15

WHEN GINGER AND JOHNNY SPOKE AGAIN

As the sun rose over the distant horizon, I carried Ginger out to my dad's landscaped, backyard garden. I sat on a chair with Ginger on my lap. I didn't know what to say. I didn't know what to think. Ginger was silent. The morning dew was quickly drying on the blades of grass so I put Ginger down.

People always told me that I look like my dad. I'm not sure about that. My dad was remarkably handsome. People always told me that I "take after" my dad. I'm not sure about that. My dad was the most honest, sincerest, kindest, gentlest, most charming and thoughtful person anyone could ever meet. My dad has been described as a Saint, and sometimes as an Angel. I'm neither. People always told me that I sound just like my dad. Okay. I'll go for that. I inherited his voice. I inherited his accent. I inherited his cadence. I inherited his sense of humor. He and I often thought alike. Johnny was my dad. Johnny was my friend. This was a big loss for me, and for every person who ever had the pleasure to know this glorified soul. Men like my dad should not be forgotten. They must be talked about, they must be remembered, so that people around the world can know that truly good people exist, and are out there. This should be an inspiration to everyone. Sometimes it is difficult to believe that men like my dad actually exist, but they do. They are all around us. We just wish they could be around for a lot longer, because we need them.

Ginger was seated on the grass. Sad. Confused. She knew what happened. She knew what was happening before I knew. She knew before my dad knew. She knew before the doctors knew. Ginger always knew.

We sat in silence for a long while. The air was getting warmer and warmer with each passing minute.

I looked up and said, "It's going to be okay."

Ginger looked at me. My voice did sound like my dad's. Maybe she thought he was speaking.

I looked down at her and smiled. I said . . .

"Johnny loves Ginger."

She stood up and looked around, but not at me.

I said it again.

"Johnny loves Ginger."

She looked around some more. She wagged her tail.

One more time I said, "Johnny loves Ginger."

She looked up at the sky. Her eyes began to sparkle.

I looked up, too. A curtain of clouds blew away.

After a moment I said, "Who does Ginger love?"

She looked up at the sky and began to bark.

Ginger barked 5 times.

Bark Bark. Bark. Bark Bark.

I wonder if she was responding to me, or did she hear something

else? Someone else? Did she hear my dad? She was looking
up as if she was seeing someone there, looking down at her. Yes.
It's true. She was looking up as if my amazing dad was talking to
her from above.

Bark Bark. Bark. Bark Bark.

And we all know what she was saying, don't we?

She was clearly saying ...

"Ginger loves Johnny."

"Ginger loves Johnny."

"Ginger loves Johnny."

I love you

Johnny Loves Ginger

I'm proud of you

Don't worry

You're a good son.

Please
help me

GINGER LOVES JOHNNY

Afterword

I am sorry to say that within one hour of looking up to the sky in the garden, **Ginger was abruptly abducted and taken from Johnny's home**. We know who took her. We also know who has her now. But that person refuses to return Ginger to me or to the estate.

As of the date of publication, we are still trying to bring Ginger home. I promised my dad I would take care of her. That is what he wanted.

Do you want to help us try to bring Ginger home? Please share this book with everyone you know, and encourage others to do so, too. If possible, please contribute, and encourage others to contribute, to the **Ginger Loves Johnny Project**. Go to CampfireNetwork.com or GingerLovesJohnny.com for more info.

Funds will be used for part of our legal battle to bring Ginger home, and to print copies of this book to be donated to schools and non-profit organizations. We also want to educate people about the importance of including their non-human companions in their estate planning.

At this time we are in the process of writing the story-behind-the-story. It will be entitled **Ginger & Johnny & Me.**

ABOUT

D.C. Blackbird is the creator of the following books: "Jekyll Says", "Jekyll Says More", "Dreaming of Kittlyand," and "Cat Heaven is Real."

Campfire Publishing is a division of the Campfire Entertainment Network, producers of audio & visual documentaries and publisher of books that showcase architectural history, design psychology, landscaping design, and books that celebrate non-human animals.

To learn more about the story of **Ginger Loves Johnny**, or to order digital and print copies, or to make a donation to the **Ginger Loves Johnny Project** to help get Ginger back home, please visit CampfireNetwork.com or GingerLovesJohnny.com

Me & my dad.

COPYRIGHT

ACKNOWLEDGMENTS

We want to thank all of our friends who have made a special effort to assist us in the publication of this book, including "the Cardinals" who provided creative exterior and interior book design ideas, and secured the artists who have contributed to the visual aspects of telling this story.

Illustrations of Johnny & Ginger by Nikola Panev.

Special thanks to many of Johnny's friends, blood-relatives, neighbors, and all those who cared about him at some point, and throughout his wonderful life. Most of all, we want to thank my dad Johnny. He was the inspiration for every positive thing I ever did. My accomplishments are his accomplishments since they would not have happened had I not been born. My dad. Wow.

GINGER LOVES JOHNNY

www.ingramcontent.com/pod-product-compliance
Lightning Source LLC
LaVergne TN
LVHW072111070426
835509LV00003B/112